# Strategic Inventions of the Napoleonic Wars

Jeri Freedman

Cavendish Square

New York

Published in 2017 by Cavendish Square Publishing, LLC
243 5th Avenue, Suite 136, New York, NY 10016

Copyright © 2017 by Cavendish Square Publishing, LLC

First Edition

Library of Congress Cataloging-in-Publication Data

Names: Freedman, Jeri, author.
Title: Strategic inventions of the Napoleonic Wars / Jeri Freedman.
Description: New York : Cavendish Square Publishing, [2017] |
Series: Tech in the trenches | Includes bibliographical references and index.
Identifiers: LCCN 2016030836 (print) | LCCN 2016034495 (ebook) |
ISBN 9781502623515 (library bound) | ISBN 9781502623522 (ebook)
Subjects: LCSH: Napoleonic Wars, 1800-1815--Technology--Juvenile literature. |
Technology--France--History--19th century--Juvenile literature. |
Inventions--France--History--19th century--Juvenile literature. |
Napoleon I, Emperor of the French, 1769-1821--Juvenile literature.
Classification: LCC DC226.4 .F74 2017 (print) | LCC DC226.4 (ebook) |
DDC 940.2/7--dc23
LC record available at https://lccn.loc.gov/2016030836

Editorial Director: David McNamara
Editor: Kristen Susienka
Copy Editor: Nathan Heidelberger
Associate Art Director: Amy Greenan
Designer: Jessica Nevins
Production Coordinator: Karol Szymczuk
Photo Researcher: J8 Media

# CONTENTS

This portrait shows Napoleon Bonaparte, aged about thirty-five, in the uniform of the first consul.

# The Napoleonic Age

The Napoleonic age occured at the border of two eras. The first was the end of the Enlightenment in the late eighteenth century—a period that marked the flowering of scientific exploration and the discovery of many scientific principles. Understanding these principles enabled unprecedented feats of engineering and invention. The second era was the beginning of the Industrial Revolution of the early nineteenth century. This time was marked by the development of machines and the rise of factories. Early industrialization signaled the beginning of the modern era, a migration from farms to cities, and a change from manual to mechanized labor. It also saw the start of the mechanization of war—the switch to standard rather than custom parts for weapons and the creation of workshops where enormous numbers of weapons were produced to supply the vast armies of the time. These developments evolved in the latter part of the nineteenth century into factories that mass-produced goods. In the Napoleonic era, for the first time, sailing ships and horse-drawn **artillery** were supplemented by vehicles that flew above the battlefield and sailed beneath the sea.

## NAPOLEON IN THE NAPOLEONIC AGE

In many ways, the most remarkable element of the Napoleonic age was its namesake, Napoleon Bonaparte. Napoleon was small of stature but heroic—and often ruthless—in his ambition. He dominated from 1799 to 1815. From the rank of a captain of artillery, he rose to become an emperor who conquered most of Europe. He was a master of military strategy and a politician adept at public relations. A student of history, he wished to create an empire like that of ancient Rome. A man of enormous ambition who refused to acknowledge any limitations, he would overreach himself in the end, and his attempt would lead to failure—but not before he had changed the world and the nature of warfare.

Napoleon was a man of contradictions. On one hand, he embraced the ideals of the French Revolution (1789–1799), especially that a man could make anything of himself if he had the will and intelligence. He believed in meritocracy—in the doctrine that the best and most capable should rise to the top. On the other hand, he raised his brothers and sisters to the status of monarchs throughout Europe. He assumed the position of dictator yet spread many of the ideals of the French Revolution across the world. His attitude toward innovation was similarly contradictory. He avidly supported inventions he thought would give him military advantage, yet he viewed scientists and inventors as dreamers and charlatans who were out to extract funds from him.

## VYING FOR POWER

The Napoleonic Wars (1803–1815) were, to a large extent, a continuation of the French Revolutionary Wars. From 1792 until Napoleon's defeat at Waterloo in 1815, France was continuously at war with a series of **coalitions** composed of various European nations. In all, there were seven coalitions. During the French Revolutionary Wars, France fought the first two. During the Napoleonic Wars, the country faced the other five.

At this time in history, the primary nation in the coalitions against France was Britain. Napoleon saw Britain as France's chief challenger for the role of the world's most dominant country. At that time, Britain had an empire and was master of trade routes that stretched not only across Europe but also throughout North Africa, the Middle East, and the Far East. This was exactly the type of dominance that Napoleon aspired to. He knew that the key to making France the preeminent power in Europe was weakening Britain's empire and damaging her trade. Although he never succeeded in significantly reducing Britain's power, this goal influenced his political decisions and choices of targets.

## IN THE FOOTSTEPS OF A REVOLUTION

When Napoleon assumed power, there was still a great deal of unrest in Paris from the French Revolution. Many people resented the government, which collected more in taxes than it spent on providing services to its citizens. People were tired of the constant chaos that marked the revolutionary years and were fed up with government incompetence and corruption. In the face of all these challenges, Napoleon—strong and heroic, victor of battle after battle—promised them stability, but without the oppressive class structure of the former feudal monarchy. He won the support of the people by trading on his popularity and had little trouble getting constitutional change after change. His military victories garnered him the support of the people and their "votes" in public referendums for the changes he proposed.

Napoleon first assumed control of the government in 1799 by **coup d'état**. Immediately following, he instituted a form of governance used by the ancient Romans he so admired—a **consulate**: three consuls elected to office for ten years. Napoleon himself was first consul. In practice, he was the one in control. Initially, he was to rule for ten years, but in 1802, by popular vote, he achieved a legislative change that altered his term to life, and finally a second referendum made him emperor in 1804.

Although known for his military achievements, Napoleon was more than a general. He instituted a number of important reforms during his rule. One was the Concordat of 1801. During the revolution, the Catholic Church had been outlawed, although religion continued to be practiced in secret. The Concordat allowed Catholicism to be once more practiced openly, but retaining the revolutionary goal of freedom of religion, it was no longer the official state religion.

Napoleon eliminated government corruption, centralized France's finances, established a system of promotion based on merit rather than class or birth, and implemented a new code of laws, referred to as the Napoleonic Code. Napoleon reorganized the governmental structure of France, with the national government at the top and the regional governments as subsidiaries under it. This made France one unified nation, in which the ministries in Paris made decisions for the entire country. Napoleon set up the first French national bank, the Bank of France.

## AN ESSENTIAL EDUCATION

Education was extremely important to Napoleon. However, he did not give equal education to both boys and girls. Instead, he focused much of his attention on reforming boys' education systems. He wanted a meritocracy in government and the military, and he saw education as the means to create the men who served. When he assumed power, he had a survey conducted of French schools. This revealed areas that lacked schools and complaints about existing schools. As a result, he upgraded the primary and secondary school systems and overhauled the university system.

Napoleon divided boys' education into two parts. Boys under age twelve were taught general knowledge such as reading, writing, history, and the use of arms. Boys over twelve were divided into two groups, those pursuing a civil career and those pursuing a career in the military. Boys studying for civil careers attended classes in languages, **rhetoric**, and philosophy. Boys pursuing military careers attended classes that stressed mathematics, physics, chemistry, and military issues. Under Napoleon's system, any boy graduating from the program was guaranteed a position in his field.

For those boys who wished to pursue careers that required education beyond secondary school, Napoleon established a series of *lycées*, which were essentially colleges with a six-year term of study. Students undertook what we would call a "liberal arts" education, studying languages, contemporary literature, science, and a variety of other subjects.

For girls, receiving an education equal to boys was not in Napoleon's plans. Many girls went to Catholic schools to learn domestic skills, such as homemaking and cooking, traits Napoleon believed would benefit girls in the future. Allowing them access to the same subjects as boys, however, was out of the question. Nevertheless, many girls did learn how to read and write and speak other languages, and some dabbled in history and some sciences, such as physics and botany.

In addition to producing educated leadership for the government and military of France, Napoleon's educational system was designed to increase the number of people in the middle class. People in the middle class tended to be more interested in

Napoleon is crowned king of Italy in Milan Cathedral.

protecting their **prosperity** than in engaging in uprisings, so a country with a healthy middle class was seen as more stable and less likely to give the government trouble.

## GOVERNING FRANCE

Napoleon's government constituted an **amalgam** of a dictatorship with the individual rights of men espoused by the French Revolution. In 1804, when Napoleon assumed the title of emperor of the French, he included the Catholic Church in the ceremony. However, when the pope raised the crown to put it on Napoleon's head, Napoleon took it and placed it on his head himself. The move was met with applause by a public that recognized what it meant: he was assuming rule on his own merit, not by the grace of God. Despite the fact that the country was no longer a **republic**, the revolution had achieved one of its key goals—people would rise by virtue of their own skill. The nobility and the Catholic Church no longer held power over them. Napoleon could rule, but only as long as he had the support of the army and the people—as the end of his reign would demonstrate.

In some ways, Napoleon was a man of his time, believing that force was the best way to institute change and that the most advanced nations had the right to impose their rule—and ideas— on other states. He believed that one homogeneous empire was preferable to a variety of independent cultures. In other ways, Napoleon was a man of the future, with the vision to see the potential for new technologies and the importance of science and engineering to military success. At times, these two sides of his personality were at war with each other. This often led him to try new devices and equipment, such as using balloons for aerial surveillance, only to abandon them or relegate them to minor support positions and return to his tried-and-true artillery and cavalry approach to warfare. Still, many innovations that were first tried in the Napoleonic era matured in the late nineteenth, twentieth, and twenty-first centuries. And Napoleon himself stands as a person who, through his actions, changed the course of history.

Today, hot-air balloons continue to be used, but for fun rather than surveillance.

This painting shows Napoleon in his role as general crossing the Saint-Bernard Pass. It was created by Jacque-Louis David.

# The Rise of a Conqueror

**M**any people consider Napoleon Bonaparte (1769–1821) to be the greatest general of all time. The techniques and tactics he used in warfare are still studied and applied today. Napoleon was an innovator, always looking for improvements that would give his army the advantage. He developed many of these weapons and tactics during the French Revolutionary Wars and continued to innovate throughout his military career as he conquered much of Europe during the Napoleonic Wars.

## WHO WAS NAPOLEON?

Napoleon Bonaparte (Napoleon I) was a French military leader who became the first emperor of France. He was born in 1769 in Ajaccio, the capital of the French-owned island of Corsica, located off the coast of Italy. His father was Carlo Buonaparte (1746–1785), a lawyer, who became Corsica's representative to the court of King Louis XVI of France. Napoleon's parents were minor members of the Corsican nobility.

In 1779, Napoleon began studying at a religious school, but after a few months, he was admitted to a military academy at Brienne-le-Château. He excelled in mathematics and did well in history and geography. After completing his studies at the military academy, he gained entrance to the École Militaire (Military School) in Paris, where he trained to become an officer in the artillery. When he graduated in 1785, he became a second lieutenant in the artillery in the French army.

In 1789, the French Revolution began. The citizens of France rose up against the French monarchy, **aristocrats**, and clergy to establish a republic. Napoleon became affiliated with the Jacobins, a leading revolutionary group, while he was on leave in Corsica. In 1792, the revolutionaries executed King Louis XVI and Queen Marie Antoinette. Having abolished the monarchy, they replaced it with a National Convention of elected representatives.

Napoleon had spent most of the first few years of the revolution in Corsica. He was a fervent Corsican nationalist who thought Corsica should rule itself. Over time, however, he became more aligned with French politics. This way of thinking resulted in a political clash with Pasquale Paoli (1725–1807), the governor of Corsica, in 1793, and Napoleon and his family fled to mainland France. Napoleon returned to military duty as a captain.

The storming of the Bastille by the citizens of France symbolized the power of the people.

# THE REVOLUTIONARY YEARS

In 1793, Napoleon wrote a pro-republican pamphlet, *Le souper de Beaucaire* (*Supper at Beaucaire*). Its publication gained him the support of Augustin Robespierre, who was the younger brother of Maximilien Robespierre, one of most important leaders of the revolution. As a result, Napoleon was appointed artillery commander of the republican forces at the Siege of Toulon (September to December 1793).

Toulon was an important port, and the revolutionary government had about one-third of its naval ships docked there. The royalists, who wanted to restore the monarchy of France, had taken control of Toulon and called on a combined British and Spanish fleet for help. In turn, the fleet sent thirteen thousand troops. If the royalists retained control of Toulon, this would cripple the French navy and encourage other areas of France to rebel against the republic.

Napoleon developed a plan to capture a hill and fortify it with guns. From that position, the French would dominate the city's harbor. His strategy led to the capture of the city and the forced evacuation of the British. At age twenty-four, Napoleon was promoted to brigadier general and put in charge of the artillery for France's Army of Italy.

On October 3, 1795, the royalists in Paris declared a rebellion against the republican legislature, the National Convention. Improvised forces had assembled in Paris to defend the National Convention, located in the Tuileries Palace. Paul Barras, a

Napoleon and his wife Josephine de Beauharnais model the plans for their coronation as emperor and empress of France.

republican leader who was aware of Napoleon's military **prowess**, put Napoleon in command, charging him with defense of the National Convention. Napoleon had observed a massacre of the Swiss Guard that had protected the king three years before, and he was aware of what was needed to ensure adequate protection. He knew that success would depend on artillery. He commandeered large cannons and used them to drive back the attackers. Fourteen hundred royalists were killed, and the rest fled. The defeat ended the royalist threat to the National Convention.

Following this, Napoleon became famous and was rewarded financially and professionally. He was given the position of commander of the interior with command of all of the French Army of Italy.

On March 9, 1796, Napoleon married Josephine de Beauharnais. Two days later he left for Italy, where he assumed command of the Army of Italy and swiftly attacked the **Piedmontese** forces, planning to defeat them before their Austrian allies could come to their aid. In rapid succession he won several victories. It took him only two weeks to defeat the Piedmontese forces, leaving him free to concentrate on the Austrian army for the balance of the war. Napoleon undertook a siege of the city of Mantua, blocking numerous efforts by the Austrians to break the siege. He triumphed at the battles of Castiglione, Bassano, and Arcole before winning a decisive victory at Rivoli in 1797. This success resulted in the total collapse of the Austrian forces in Italy.

The focus of the war then turned to southern Germany. In 1796, Austrians led by Archduke Charles, Duke of Teschen, defeated French forces. However, one year later, in the first major clash between the archduke and Napoleon, Napoleon pushed Austrian forces back and won the Battle of Tarvis in March, advancing deep into Austrian territory and coming within 62 miles (100 kilometers) of Vienna. The Austrians sued for peace. The Treaties of Leoben and Campo Formio ceded control of northern Italy, the Netherlands, and Belgium to France, areas that had been controlled by Austria. A secret clause promised the Republic of Venice to Austria. After the Treaty of Campo Formio was signed, Napoleon attacked Venice and forced it into submission.

## MILITARY STRATEGY

In planning his battle strategy, Napoleon relied heavily on artillery. Given his background as an artillery officer, he was well aware of the advantages that artillery could provide. One of the innovations that occurred in the French army during the French Revolutionary Wars was the introduction of mobile artillery, which was lighter and easier to move, allowing it to be deployed more easily by both infantry and cavalry soldiers. Most generals of the time relied primarily on infantry to fight battles, and they used artillery to support the foot soldiers by driving back enemy forces or knocking down fortifications. Napoleon pioneered the use of artillery as a primary means of attack, using massed artillery to charge enemy lines with a barrage of projectiles and shells, and then attacking the surviving enemy.

In earlier eras, armies would line up in rows opposite each other and then attack, head-to-head. Napoleon instead broke his force into discrete units, which would attack from the flanks, or sides. Often he would conceal his troops' location. Then, after the front had been softened by an artillery attack, the units would storm the weakened enemy from multiple points. Napoleon would often take the central position at the hinge point between two cooperating enemy units, attacking one until it retreated and then swinging around to fight the other. As a result of his technology and strategy, Napoleon's army won eighteen battles, took 150,000 enemy soldiers prisoner, and accumulated a great deal of loot during the Italian campaign. His troops took approximately $45 million in cash and about $12 million in jewels and precious metals. They also captured more than three hundred valuable pieces of art.

Napoleon knew the value of publicity as well as technology. He founded two newspapers, one for circulation to his troops, the other for general circulation in France.

## THE DICTATOR'S PATH

In 1797, the royalist faction had a majority of seats in the French legislature. Fearing that Napoleon was accumulating a war chest to lead a coup to set himself up as dictator of France, they attacked him. The republicans feared the royalists' increasing power. Paul Barras, Jean-François Rewbell, and Louis Marie de La Révellière-Lépeaux, three members of the Directory, the new legislative branch of the French government, appealed to Napoleon, commander of the interior, for assistance. Napoleon sent General Pierre Augereau to Paris to support them. On September 4, 1797, they staged a coup d'état in which they took control of the government and purged the royalists.

Although the republicans were once again firmly in control of France, the directors were now dependent on Napoleon to stay in power. Napoleon concluded a peace treaty, the Treaty of Campo Formio, with the Austrians and returned a hero to Paris in December 1797. In conjunction with France's foreign minister, Charles Maurice de Talleyrand-Périgord (more commonly known as Talleyrand; 1754–1838), he began to develop a plan to invade Britain.

After spending several months in 1798 invading and then being driven out of Egypt—except for a few French strongholds—in 1799, Napoleon and the French suffered a series of military defeats in Europe. The Directory sent Napoleon instructions to return to France to defend the country against possible invasion. Because of the poor lines of communication between France and Egypt, Napoleon didn't get the order. However, he had learned of the military situation in Europe from his own sources, and in August 1799, he set off for France. By the time he arrived in Paris in October 1799, the military situation had reversed, with the French winning a series of victories. Despite the failure of the French in the Middle East, Napoleon was greeted in France as a hero. He formed an alliance that included his brother Lucien; two of the directors of the republic, Joseph Fouché and Emmanuel Joseph

# The Egyptian Expedition

Napoleon and his army were the dominant military force on land. However, they were less imposing at sea. The British navy was the most powerful in the world, and Napoleon knew that his forces would be at a disadvantage if they challenged them. This was apparent during the next campaign.

In May 1798, Napoleon set off on an expedition to conquer Egypt. The expedition's goal was to **undermine** Britain's trade with India by cutting off Egypt and establishing a French presence in the Middle East. He then hoped to form an alliance with Sultan Tipu, an enemy of the British in India. Napoleon promised the Directory that once he had taken Egypt, he would establish relations with the Indian princes and jointly attack the English in India.

Because he believed the French navy was not yet up to a confrontation with the British navy, Napoleon sailed to Egypt using a different route, designed to avoid detection by the British. It worked, and he arrived in Alexandria, Egypt, on July 1, 1798. Shortly after, he won the Battle of Shubra Khit against Egypt's ruling military caste, the Mamluks. He followed up that victory by winning the Battle of the Pyramids on July 21.

Eventually, however, the British navy, under the command of Admiral Horatio Nelson, did locate the French **flotilla** of ships. Nelson attacked and defeated the French in the Battle of the Nile, capturing or sinking all but two French ships. The defeat put an end to Napoleon's attempt to disrupt British control of the Middle East, although the French did retain some control in Egypt. The need for a better way to challenge the British navy ultimately led Napoleon to hire Robert Fulton in 1800 to design a submarine.

Sieyès; Roger Ducos, speaker of the Council of Five Hundred (the lower house of the legislature at the time); and Talleyrand. On November 9, 1799, Napoleon conducted a coup d'état.

On that day, Sieyès, in his role as speaker of the upper house of the legislature, arranged for both the upper and lower houses to meet on the following day in the palace in Saint-Cloud, France— supposedly for safety from a plot against the legislature in Paris. In reality, it was merely a ploy to get the legislature away from Paris and into an area controlled by Napoleon's troops.

The next day, the legislators became suspicious after hearing rumors and observing troops in the area. But before they could react, the conspirators called in soldiers. Napoleon's confederates forced the legislature to declare an end to the Directory and the creation of a new government, headed by Napoleon. Mirroring the form of government of ancient Rome, the government was to be led by three consuls, of whom Napoleon was decreed to be the first consul, aided by consuls Sieyès and Roger Ducos. The legislature was dissolved, and in November 1799, Napoleon took up residence in the Tuileries Palace in Paris. Napoleon's position was confirmed by a new constitution, the Constitution of the Year VIII. It was designed to maintain the impression that France was a republic, with Napoleon being appointed first consul for ten years. In reality, Napoleon became the dictator of France.

Napoleon crosses the Alps with the French Reserve Army in the spring of 1800.

Strategic Inventions of the Napoleonic Wars

## FRENCH CONSULATE

One of Napoleon's actions upon assuming the position of first consul was to clean up the military mess in Europe. In the spring of 1800, he and an army crossed the Swiss Alps into Italy, with the intention of taking back the Italian peninsula, which the Austrians had recaptured while Napoleon was engaged in Egypt. He made the audacious move of invading from the north over the Alps, which meant a difficult crossing, rather than taking the easier and more common approach from the western coast. He led his troops into northern Italy unopposed, while the Austrian army was occupied besieging another branch of the French army, commanded by André Masséna, duke of Rivoli (1758–1817). The continued resistance of Masséna's troops in the south gave the northern army time to prepare for engagement with the Austrian army, which was commanded by General Michael Friedrich Benedikt, Baron von Melas (1729–1806).

The French and Austrian armies met at the Battle of Marengo on June 14, 1800. The French were outnumbered by about six thousand soldiers. The Austrians initially surprised the French troops, and their attack forced the French to retreat. Believing he had won, General Melas retired to his quarters that afternoon, leaving **subordinates** in charge. The French retreat was a tactical move, however. Late in the afternoon, French reinforcement troops reached the battlefield. Napoleon initiated a series of artillery barrages and cavalry charges that decimated the Austrian army, leaving fourteen thousand Austrian soldiers dead. The Austrian troops fled to Alessandria in Piedmont, Italy. The next day, the Austrian army consented to the Convention of Alessandria. They agreed to abandon northern Italy, and the army was guaranteed safe passage to friendly soil in return for turning over their fortresses in the area.

The triumph at Marengo solidified Napoleon's political authority at home and increased his popular support. The final word was not in, however. Although the Austrian army had agreed to give up northern Italy, the government of Austria had not, and they would not acknowledge that the territory belonged to France. When it became clear that negotiations had reached an **impasse**, Napoleon ordered the French army, under Jean Victor Marie Moreau (1763–1813), to attack Austria once again. The

French swept through Bavaria and in December 1800 achieved a definitive victory at Hohenlinden. The Austrians surrendered, and in February 1801 they signed the Treaty of Lunéville.

In 1802, Britain, the last country at war with France, signed the Treaty of Amiens. After nearly ten years of battles, the French Revolutionary Wars came to a close. In the treaty, Britain agreed to withdraw from the colonial territories they'd recently conquered, and France agreed to stop its attempts to expand into new territories.

With peace came increasing economic prosperity. Napoleon's popularity soared. In the spring of 1802, he called for a vote on a new constitution, which was overwhelmingly approved by the people of France. The new constitution made the consulate a permanent institution, instead of one lasting for ten years. The result was that Napoleon was now dictator for life.

The British fleet at the Battle of Trafalgar, October 21, 1805, led by Admiral Nelson's flagship, *Victoria*, painted by Norman Wilkinson

# The Napoleonic Wars

The Napoleonic Wars (1803–1815) were a continuation of the French Revolutionary Wars. Despite the brief peace after Napoleon became emperor of France, it was not long before a new coalition of European countries formed to challenge the French empire. This coalition was merely the third of what would ultimately be seven. The first two coalitions had challenged France during the French Revolutionary Wars.

## PRELUDE TO WAR

Although Britain and France signed the Treaty of Amiens in 1802, ending the French Revolutionary Wars, neither side truly abided by its terms. Napoleon did not give up his ambitions for France. He annexed Piedmont and Elba, declared himself president of the Italian Republic, and maintained control of the Netherlands.

Britain refused to withdraw its troops from the island of Malta, which it had seized during the French Revolutionary Wars, and declined to withdraw its troops from Egypt, fearing French disruption of its trade routes in the Middle East. France had withdrawn from Switzerland at the end of the Revolutionary Wars, after setting up a republican government, but after the withdrawal, violence broke out between pro- and antigovernment groups. In 1802, Napoleon again invaded the country and occupied it. His actions outraged the British. They retaliated by refusing to return the Cape Colony (part of present-day South Africa) to the Netherlands, as they had agreed to do in the Treaty of Amiens.

In early 1803, Britain issued a demand to France that Britain be allowed to retain Malta for ten years. Malta would have provided the French with a convenient location from which to invade Egypt, so the British needed it to protect their trade routes. The British also demanded the island of Lampedusa, which was owned by the Kingdom of Sicily, and required that the French evacuate the Netherlands. In return, they offered to recognize the French control of Italy, if the French left Switzerland and paid the king of Sardinia for the territory he'd lost to the French. In response, France proposed that Russia control Malta, to ease British fears of French control, and said that France would evacuate the Netherlands when the British left Malta. France, in addition, offered to convene a convention to address the other British concerns. None of these efforts to maintain peace between France and Britain resolved the issues, however, and on May 18, 1803, Britain declared war on France.

# THE WAR OF THE THIRD COALITION

A major motivation for Britain's declaration of war on France in 1803 was Napoleon's ambitions to control all of Europe. This fact posed both a physical and financial threat to Britain. If Napoleon gained control of mainland Europe, it would only be a matter of time before he attacked Britain. Further, the more areas Napoleon controlled in Europe, the better position he would be in to interfere with Britain's trade routes and colonies, which Britain relied on for resources and goods. The rise of France's influence in Europe was also a blow to Britain's pride because Britain, with its vast empire, was arguably the most powerful country in the world up to that point.

Napoleon considered mounting an invasion of Britain. However, before he could make such a move, he needed to address the fact that the French navy could not best the British navy. Without new technologies, his fleet would be at the mercy of the British.

Napoleon came up with a complicated plan to draw the British fleet away from the English Channel, which separates England from France. The plan relied on threatening the British colonies in the West Indies, which would require the British to sail their navy there in defense. This effort failed, however, because the Franco-Spanish fleet was forced to withdraw to the southern Spanish city of Cádiz after a confrontation with the British Royal Navy at Cape Finisterre, along the western coast of Spain, on July 22, 1805. The Royal Navy went on to **blockade** Cádiz. The French fleet left Cádiz and headed for Naples on October 19, 1805, but the Royal

Navy caught them and completely defeated them in the Battle of Trafalgar on October 21. The conflict represented Napoleon's last attempt to engage the British in a naval battle.

Meanwhile, Britain had gathered allies to form the Third Coalition against France. Earlier that year, in April 1805, she had signed a treaty with Russia. Both countries agreed to work together to drive the French from the Netherlands and Switzerland. After Napoleon annexed Genoa and declared himself king of Italy in March 1805, Austria joined the British-Russian coalition. Sweden joined the coalition in August that same year.

After joining the coalition, the Austrians invaded Bavaria. The French Army arrived in Ulm in September to meet them. The Battle of Ulm took place from September 25 to October 20, 1805. Napoleon ultimately surrounded the Austrian army and forced it to surrender. Having defeated the only part of the Austrian army in northern Europe, Napoleon went on to occupy Vienna, the capital of Austria. He met the much larger Austro-Russian army at Austerlitz in Moravia. In what is often considered his greatest triumph, Napoleon definitively defeated the larger Austro-Russian army on December 2, 1805. The Austrians and Russians suffered twenty-five thousand casualties, while the French lost only seven thousand men. On December 26, 1805, Austria signed the Treaty of Pressburg with France. Under the treaty, Austria was required to surrender Venice to the Kingdom of Italy and give the Tyrol to Bavaria. With the signing of the treaty, Austria withdrew from the coalition. Napoleon now controlled Belgium, the Netherlands, Switzerland, most of western Germany, and northern Italy.

In 1806, the British attempted to make peace with France. The British proposed that they would keep the foreign areas they had conquered and that Hanover would be restored to the British king, George III. In return, they would agree to accept French ownership of the areas Napoleon had conquered in Europe. The French were willing to let the British have Malta, the Cape Colony, the island of Tobago, and the French-held areas of India, but they wanted to be given Sicily in return for letting Britain have Hanover. Negotiations fell apart when the British refused.

On May 16, 1806, the British used their navy to blockade the coasts of France. Napoleon, in turn, issued the Berlin Decree, which prohibited French territories from trading with Britain. The decree created the **Continental System**, a policy whereby French-controlled European states could trade only with other European states on the continent, not with Britain. At this time, half of Britain's army of 220,000 was engaged in securing the colonies and Ireland, and in protecting England from possible attack. Therefore, Britain could only send 110,000 troops into a foreign war. France, in contrast, had 2.5 million full- and part-time soldiers. There is no doubt that the French had superior land forces, and the British had superior naval forces. The Royal Navy interfered with France's foreign trade by seizing its ships and keeping foreign vessels from entering French ports. However, it couldn't do anything to keep France from trading over land with other European nations.

# The Military-Industrial Complex

The military-industrial complex arose during the Napoleonic Wars. It referred to a close relationship between the military and industries that produce weapons or armament. One of the changes that brought about the Napoleonic Wars was a change in the nature of warfare itself. Prior to the Napoleonic Wars, most conflicts were fought between monarchies, often only between two countries. Armies were small, often supplied by nobility from the populations of the lands they controlled.

The Napoleonic Wars were fought using much larger numbers of people. Armies had hundreds of thousands of soldiers (sometimes, as in the case of France, more than one million), and many civilians on the home front produced weapons and supplies in big workshops (early forms of factories). Thus, war had a significant effect on the economy. The increase in the size of military forces and the improvements in military technology meant that invading forces and the effects of war transformed the lives of all of the populace. For the first time, nations engaged in "total war." During this period, the military emerged as a major segment of the economy.

Workers in a French weapons factory workshop make rifles.

## THE WAR OF THE FOURTH COALITION

In July 1806, just months after the Third Coalition collapsed, Britain formed alliances with Prussia, Saxony, and Sweden to create the Fourth Coalition (1806–1807). In August 1806, Frederick William III (1770–1840), the Prussian king, declared war on France independently. On October 8, 1806, Napoleon attacked Prussia at Jena. On October 14, 1806, Napoleon and his army won the Battle of Jena. A second force led by General Louis-Nicholas Davout, duke of Auerstadt (1770–1823), defeated the Prussian forces at Auerstadt. In all, 160,000 French soldiers attacked Prussia and killed 25,000 Prussian soldiers and captured 150,000 out of a total army of 250,000. The city-state of Saxony left Prussia and allied itself with France, as did several other small states from north Germany. Napoleon combined these states of north and western Germany into the Confederation of the Rhineland to make ruling the area easier.

The French went on to force the Russians out of Poland. Napoleon's forces fought the Russians in the Battle of Eylau (February 7–8, 1807), but the result was a stalemate. However, the French forces beat the Russians at the Battle of Danzig on May 24, 1807, and the Battle of Hellsberg on July 10, 1807. As a result of these losses, the Russians withdrew to the north. Napoleon confronted them at Friedland on June 14, 1807, and soundly defeated the Russian forces. New states were formed in Germany and Poland, including the Kingdom of Westphalia, the Republic of Danzig, and the Duchy of Warsaw.

# THE WAR OF THE FIFTH COALITION

In 1809, France was engaged in the Peninsular War on the **Iberian Peninsula**, fighting Spain and Portugal. Britain formed the Fifth Coalition, which consisted of Britain and Austria. The sea became a major theater of war against Napoleon's allies. Britain used its navy to good effect and scored a number of successes against France's colonies. The Peninsular War began because Napoleon found that Spain and Portugal were continuing to let British goods into Europe, despite the Continental System. His invasion resulted in the dissolution of the France-Spain alliance. Initially, France suffered defeat in several conflicts in Spain. However, Napoleon ultimately defeated the Spanish and forced the British army to withdraw from the Iberian Peninsula.

While Napoleon was occupied in Spain, Austria decided to try to take back the German provinces that belonged to it prior to the Battle of Austerlitz. The French army continued to suffer from Spanish guerrilla attacks, and in the midst of the fighting, Napoleon had to leave Spain to deal with Austria's incursions into the French-controlled German provinces.

The British then sent Sir Arthur Wellesley (later the Duke of Wellington) to Spain with a new army. The French didn't return to the Iberian Peninsula. The Peninsular War was costly for France in terms of both money and morale.

At the Battle of Raszyn on April 19, 1809, the Austrians were defeated by the Duchy of Warsaw. At the Battle of Aspern-Essling on May 21–22, 1809, Napoleon tried to cross the Danube River near Vienna, but the Austrians, under the command of Archduke Charles, forced the French back. The battle was the first time in a decade that Napoleon was defeated. He was able to withdraw most of his forces safely, however, and at the Battle of Wagram, on July 5–6, he again crossed the Danube and engaged the Austrians. He attacked with 165,000 French, German, and Italian troops, who faced an Austrian force of 145,000 men.

The huge number of soldiers on the battlefield and the heavy use of artillery made the battle particularly bloody. Napoleon won, and the Austrians were sufficiently disheartened, signing the Treaty of Schönbrunn, in which they gave up further territories to the French.

Most of the British efforts in the War of the Fifth Coalition were naval endeavors. The Royal Navy controlled the sea, trapping France's remaining naval forces in French-controlled ports. The British did engage in some hit-and-run land attacks, but these were concentrated in areas around French-controlled ports. Such raids were mainly carried out to disrupt French supplies and communications.

## THE END OF THE EMPIRE

The War of the Sixth Coalition took place from March 1813 to March 1814. During this time, France faced a coalition consisting of Britain, Austria, Prussia, Russia, Portugal, Spain, and a number of German states. Major battles included the Battles of Lützen, Bautzen, and Dresden. The conflict culminated in the Battle of Leipzig, also called the Battle of Nations, the largest European

# Food and War

In 1812, at the height of his power, Napoleon invaded Russia with a pan-European Grande Armée (Grand Army), consisting of 650,000 men. There were 270,000 Frenchmen and thousands of soldiers from allied or subject areas. From August 16 to 18, 1812, he fought, and eventually won, the Battle of Smolensk.

At the same time, another branch of the French army, commanded by Marshal Nicolas Oudinot, was blocked by the Russian army in the Battle of Polotsk. The French, as a result, were unable to execute their plan to march on the Russian capital of St. Petersburg. Instead, Napoleon followed the Russian army, which retreated toward Moscow.

As they retreated, the Russians engaged in scorched-earth tactics, destroying everything that could be useful to the French army, including crops and livestock. Since the armies of Napoleon's day were responsible for procuring their own food by **foraging** from the land they marched through or buying it from locals, the French soldiers found themselves starving.

Without mercy, the Russians used Cossack cavalry to attack the French column en route to Moscow. The French and Russian armies finally met in the Battle of Borodino, near Moscow, on September 7, 1812. Napoleon captured some key positions but was unable to destroy the Russian army.

On September 14, Napoleon advanced into Moscow. Czar Alexander I refused to surrender the city, and peace talks failed. Faced with a stalemate, Napoleon began the disastrous Great Retreat from Moscow. By winter, as the French retreated through Russia's barren areas, only 27,000 of the 380,000 soldiers who had entered

Russia were still with the army. The rest had been killed or captured, had perished of starvation or disease, or had deserted. Napoleon's experience in Russia highlights the difficulty of having an army rely on "living off the land" for the food it needs and extending itself across a distance that requires long supply lines that can be cut by the enemy.

The French army engages in the Battle of Smolensk during the invasion of Russia during the Napoleonic Wars.

battle prior to World War I. Having been decisively defeated, Napoleon was forced to return to France, allowing the coalition to advance toward France. After a short battle, the coalition entered Paris on March 30, 1814. A few weeks later, on April 11, 1814, Napoleon was forced to **abdicate** as emperor and was sent into **exile** on the island of Elba. The coalition restored the monarchy, placing Louis XVIII on the throne.

However, that was not the end of Napoleon's story. Nearly a year later, on March 20, 1815, he escaped from Elba and returned to Paris. He reestablished himself as ruler and governed for a period called the Hundred Days. He accrued an army of 200,000 men and vowed to attack Britain and Prussia. On June 18, 1815, Napoleon met the combined armies of Britain and Prussia (the Seventh Coalition) in the Battle of Waterloo. The British army was commanded by the Duke of Wellington, and the Prussian army by Gebhard Leberecht von Blücher, Prince of Wahlstatt.

Unfortunately for him, Napoleon was firmly defeated. He abdicated a second time, in favor of his son, Napoleon II, but his son's rule went unacknowledged (he was only four years old), and Napoleon was exiled, this time to the island of St. Helena off the west coast of Africa. He remained there until his death in 1821.

French and British soldiers fight each other during the Battle of Waterloo on June 18, 1815.

This French woodcut, called *French Project for the Invasion of England in the Time of Napoleon Bonaparte*, illustrates the concept of using balloons for the invasion.

# Aerial Surveillance: Balloons and Airships

**B**eing able to fly over the battlefield or an area where an enemy is preparing for battle has obvious advantages. It allows an army to learn of an enemy's strength and weaponry. It also provides detailed information about the terrain and the enemy's location in it. During the Napoleonic Wars, the French used balloons for aerial reconnaissance, observing and transmitting military information. They employed aerial reconnaissance for the first time during the conflict with Austria in the French Revolutionary Wars and continued to do so for the first part of Napoleon's rule.

# THE DEVELOPMENT OF THE HOT-AIR BALLOON

The hot-air balloon was invented by brothers Joseph (1740–1810) and Étienne (1745–1799) Montgolfier. After encountering works by scientists such as Joseph Priestley, who proposed that gases lighter than air might be used to raise objects off the ground, Étienne proposed to his brother that they experiment with developing a balloon. The brothers tested various gases, including hydrogen (then known as "inflammable air" because of its tendency to **ignite**). They ultimately settled on plain hot air, created by burning a combination of straw and chopped-up wood. Starting with small silk balloons tested indoors, they then moved on to larger outdoor balloons. On June 4, 1783, they succeeded in the first public demonstration, getting a balloon made of cloth-lined paper to rise 3,000 feet (914 meters) and remain in the air for about ten minutes before descending in a controlled manner on a nearby hill.

The work of the Montgolfiers led others to try their own experiments. A professor of physics named J. A. C. Charles (1746–1823) created a balloon 12 feet (3.66 m) in diameter. Aware that hot air had only twice the lifting power of regular air, he decided to use hydrogen gas. He coated a balloon made of taffeta cloth with a varnish that would make it impermeable to hydrogen. On August 27, 1783, he demonstrated it in Paris, and it remained aloft for forty-five minutes.

The Montgolfiers improved their balloon by adding a straw basket and a continuous fire to keep the balloon filled with hot

The Montgolfier brothers' first manned hot-air balloon tethered off at the garden of the Reveillon workshop, Paris.

air. On November 21, 1783, Jean-François Pilâtre de Rozier, the Marquis d'Arlândes, and Gerond de Villette became the first people to fly in a hot-air balloon, crossing the city of Paris.

## MILITARY MIGHT

The military potential of an airborne machine was apparent from the beginning of the successful experiments with balloons. In 1783, Gerond de Villette wrote to the *Journal de Paris*, saying that the balloon would be useful in war for discovering the position and movements of the enemy, and for signaling this information to the army. But the French government would not express interest in such an idea for another decade.

In 1794, a French engineer named Jean-Marie-Joseph Coutelle demonstrated a balloon. He found that, from the balloon, he could use a telescope to clearly make out details as far as 18 miles (29 km) away. The French Republic at the time was ruled by the Committee of Public Safety. They had set up a commission to evaluate the utility of the balloon in war. The members of the commission were so impressed that they recommended the formation of an air force—the world's first—called the Compagnie d'Aeronautiers (company of aeronauts, or "air sailors"), also referred to as the French Aerostatic Corps. It was established on March 29, 1794, and a military balloon school was formed in the same year. It would remain in operation until 1800.

The Committee of Public Safety set up a secret balloon-experimenting facility in the suburbs of Paris. There, Coutelle, assisted by N. J. Conté, constructed the first military observation balloon, called *L'Entrepremant* (*The Enterprise*). The balloon was 30 feet (9.1 m) in diameter. It used hydrogen gas and was strong enough to withstand buffeting by wind because it was **tethered** in place. Two cables anchored it to guarantee that it wouldn't drift away if the enemy cut one cable. The balloon was manned by two people, one to control the balloon, and the other to observe the battlefield and then send messages to the generals on the ground. The messages were placed in sandbags with attached rings that allowed them to slide down one of the balloon's cables to the ground. The person communicating with the ground could also use flags to signal those below.

The newly created balloon corps transported the balloon to Mauberge in northern France, near the Belgian border. Using a telescope while stationed in the balloon's basket above Mauberge, Coutelle and Conté spied on Dutch and Austrian troops. From their vantage point, they were able to provide the French generals with details about the makeup and location of the enemy. They also helped direct artillery fire from ground units. The Austrians tried to shoot down *L'Entrepremant*, but Coutelle let out additional cable, and it rose higher, out of range.

From Mauberge, a twenty-four-man team moved the still-inflated balloon to a new location, Charleroi, Belgium, where it played a major role in the ensuing Battle of Fleurus on June 26, 1794. Coutelle and General Morlot spent the entire ten-hour battle aloft in the balloon. Questions from those on the ground and responses, orders, and reconnaissance information were sent up and down via the balloon's cables. For the first time in war, operations on the ground were directed from the air. In addition to its practical advantages, the balloon intimidated the Austrian troops.

*L'Entrepremant* was so successful that by 1796 three more balloons were constructed: the *Celeste,* the *Hercule,* and the *Intrepide.* Each balloon was used at a different front, and each was manned by its own corps of aeronauts. The balloon corps played a role in the evacuation of Mannheim, providing reconnaissance information about the location of enemy troops, which allowed the French to block or evade them. The balloons continued to perform reconnaissance in subsequent battles in Europe. The effectiveness of the balloon corps and the usefulness of the information they provided led Napoleon to agree with Coutelle that balloon corps should be part of the troops he took to Egypt in 1797.

In 1798, at the Battle of Aboukir, the British fleet destroyed the equipment. However, the French found local craftsmen who could make replacement equipment, and the balloon corps remained active.

The balloon corps in Europe was disbanded in 1799. However, the balloon corps remained in Egypt, not disbanding until it returned to France in 1802. In 1803, when Napoleon was planning his invasion of Britain, he did consider using balloons to carry troops across the English Channel and land in Britain. He went as far as to appoint Marie Madeline Sophie Blanchard as chief of the air service. However, she said the proposed air invasion wouldn't succeed because of the winds. This did not stop the rumors circulating in Britain that the French planned an aerial invasion using balloons.

## DISADVANTAGES

The big drawback with balloons was controlling their travel in the air. The French experimented with attaching wings and a **rudder** to the balloons, effectively turning them into **dirigibles**, or **blimps**, but they were not able to construct a successful version. In 1783, a lieutenant of engineers named J. B. M. Meusnier (1754–1793) wrote a paper, *Atlas des dessins relatifs a un projet de machine aerostatique* (An atlas of designs relating to an aerostatic machine project), that was published in a book in 1794. He described the construction of a 260-foot-long (79-meter-long) dirigible that was controlled by three hand-turned air screws. Unfortunately for the history of aviation, Meusnier was killed at the siege of Mainz in 1793. Although the dirigible was never built by the French, many experts believe his work formed the basis for the development of dirigibles in the nineteenth century.

Ironically, if Napoleon had still had the balloon corps at the Battle of Waterloo, where he was finally defeated by the British, he would have been able to observe the distribution of Wellington's troops, and that might have made a difference in the outcome of the battle. However, that was not the last time the world heard of reconnaissance balloons. They would reappear during the reign of Napoleon I's nephew, Napoleon III, during the Franco-Austrian War in 1859 and the Franco-Prussian War in 1870.

## The First Parachute Jump

Eighteenth-century France not only developed the first vehicle for aerial surveillance but also was the site of the first parachute jump. The Renaissance inventor Leonardo da Vinci developed the idea of a parachute, which he noted in his writings, although he never made and used one. The technology was not proved practical until 1792, when André-Jacques Garnerin (1769–1823) started designing and testing parachutes. When he came up with the idea, Garnerin was a prisoner of war in a Hungarian prison, where he was held for three years. He had the idea that one could use air resistance (the force generated by air pressing upward on a falling body) to slow a person's fall from a height—such as the ramparts of the prison. He never actually tried to make such a parachute in prison, but the idea continued to intrigue him. He constructed his first parachute in 1797. It consisted of a canopy that was 23 feet (7 m) in diameter attached to a basket with suspension lines.

Garnerin made his first jump on October 22, 1797. He attached the parachute to a hydrogen balloon and rode the balloon to an altitude of 3,200 feet (975 m). Next, he climbed from the balloon into the basket attached to the parachute and cut the lines that attached it to the balloon. He swung wildly as he fell because he hadn't put an air vent in the canopy. However, he landed safely and unhurt. He wasn't the only member of the family interested in parachuting. In 1799, Garnerin's wife, Jeanne-Genevieve, made history as the first woman to make a parachute jump.

*Opposite*: André-Jacques Garnerin releases the hot-air balloon from the basket and floats to earth with a parachute.

DESCENTE DE JACQUES GARNERIN
EN PARACHUTE (1797)

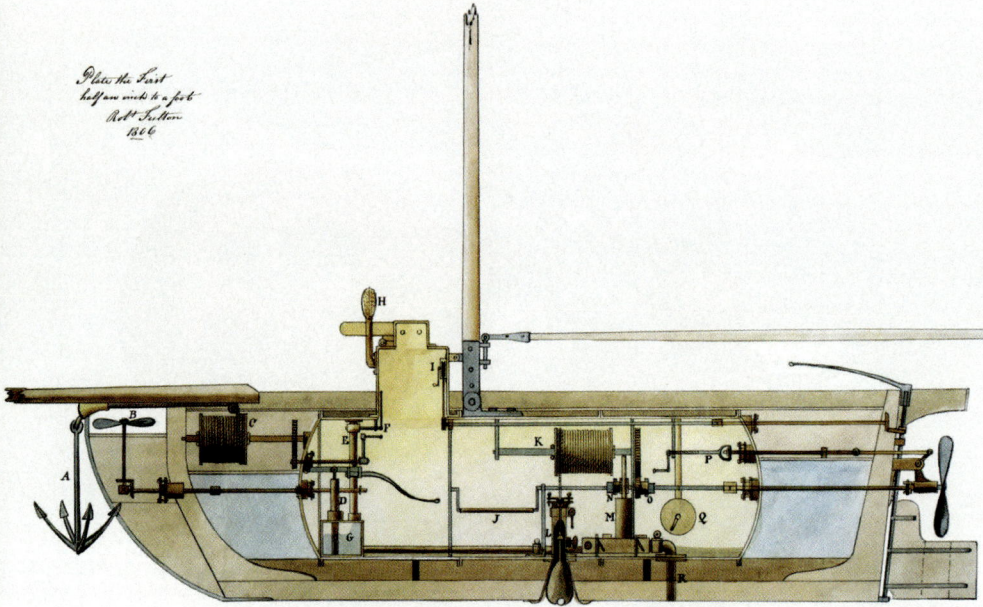

Drawn by Robert Fulton, this cross section shows the design of a submarine from 1806.

Strategic Inventions of the Napoleonic Wars

# Advances in Naval Technology: Submarines and Steamships

In the early part of the Napoleonic Wars, squadrons of ships sailed from French ports. From 1808 onward, however, the British navy came to dominate the seas. They blockaded key French ports, which made it difficult for the French to receive goods from abroad or to send supplies by ships to their armies in the field. Control of the ports also allowed the British to export goods to Europe, despite France's efforts to block British commerce. One of Napoleon's ambitions was to invade Britain. The problem the French faced was how to deal effectively with the British navy.

## ROBERT FULTON AND
## THE FRENCH NAVY

Robert Fulton (1765–1815) was an American inventor who lived in France in the late eighteenth and early nineteenth centuries. He was an engineer with a great interest in canal boats and in developing steam-powered vessels. In 1797, he went to Paris, a center of the engineering industry, and began to experiment with submarines and torpedo boats. Fulton designed the first functional submarine. He dubbed the vessel the *Nautilus* and demonstrated it by staying underwater for seventeen minutes in 25 feet (7.6 m) of water.

In 1800, Napoleon commissioned Fulton to construct a submarine. He had it built at the Perrier shipyard in Rouen. In July 1800, it sailed successfully in the Seine River. It was driven by two men, who manually turned a crank that powered the propeller. Fulton demonstrated the vessel's utility by pursuing a pair of British ships near shore. He saw the potential of the submarine as a vehicle for sailing under enemy vessels and attaching powder charges, called mines, to the bottoms of the ships.

## NAVAL ADVANCES

After successfully proving the viability of a submarine, Fulton submitted to Napoleon a plan for crossing the channel by submarine and using it to lay mines in British harbors. When Napoleon asked to see the submarine, Fulton told him it had been scrapped, but that a better model could be built if the government

## The Plot to Rescue Napoleon by Submarine

After his defeat at Waterloo, Napoleon was exiled to the island of St. Helena. While there, Napoleon lived in Longwood, a mansion in a remote part of the island, which was guarded by 2,800 soldiers and five hundred cannons. Visitors were allowed only during the day and were searched before being allowed entry. Despite the seeming impossibility of freeing Napoleon, there were a number of attempts to do so. One plan involved the use of the newly developed steamboat, and another would have made use of a balloon.

One such rescue plan was hatched by an Irish smuggler named Tom Johnson. Around 1820, he claimed that he was offered £40,000 (the equivalent of $4.4 million today) to rescue Napoleon. According to him, the plan had relied on two submarines, which he would build. The smaller would be used to pick up Napoleon, who would then be transferred to the larger. The larger submarine would submerge and plant mines beneath any ships that pursued them. It's doubtful that Johnson's idea ever got beyond the planning stage. However, a French general, the Marquis de Montholon, who went into exile with Napoleon, did write, years later, that a group of French officers planned to use a submarine to rescue Napoleon, and paid £9,000 for the ship (about $1 million today).

This is a portrait of Robert Fulton, the inventor who revolutionized naval warfare with his designs for submarines and steamships.

Strategic Inventions of the Napoleonic Wars

provided funds. This led Napoleon to state that Fulton was a charlatan trying to con the government out of money.

Fulton went on to build a steamship in the early 1800s. His first attempt was unsuccessful, but by August 1803, a new vessel sailed the waters of the Seine without mishap. The steamship was a potentially revolutionary innovation in naval technology because, unlike sailing ships, it wasn't dependent on the winds and tides. It could travel at will, even in calm seas.

Napoleon had considered invading Britain in 1798. French troops were massed on the French coast near the English Channel, but any attempt to invade Britain was put on hold when Napoleon decided to embark on a campaign in Egypt. In 1802, the peace treaty of Amiens supposedly ended hostilities between the two nations. However, in 1803, when conflict was renewed, Napoleon once again began planning an invasion. From 1803 to 1805, Napoleon amassed an army of two hundred thousand men, alternately called *Armée des côtes de l'Océan* (Army of the Ocean Coasts) or *Armée d'Angleterre* (Army of England). Napoleon also ordered the building of barges on the coasts of France and the Netherlands facing the English Channel. These would be used to transport the troops across the channel.

The British could see the French flotilla and the military encampment at Boulogne, across the channel from the south coast of England. In the coastal areas at risk from a French attack, new fortifications were built and existing ones reinforced. The defense of the British coast was the responsibility of the Royal Navy, which also patrolled the English Channel with squadrons of ships, in case the French tried to invade with barges carrying troops and equipment. The navy ships were supplemented by seagoing members of the home guard, who had regular jobs but were available to man small gun boats along the coast, in case of threat.

In 1803, Fulton submitted a second plan to Napoleon, this time for steamboats that could be used to pull barges with troops and equipment across the channel. Napoleon was still skeptical. But in July 1804, faced with the difficulties involved in getting a flotilla across the channel, he changed his mind. Fulton's steamboat scheme was resubmitted to Napoleon by the head of his marine department. Napoleon responded, "I have just read the project of Citizen Fulton, which you have sent me much too late, since it is one that may change the face of the world." He then ordered the creation of a commission to examine the plan's feasibility. However, it *was* too late for the French navy to take advantage of Fulton's work. Fulton had adopted a false identity as "Mr. Francis" and left France for London, changing sides in the conflict.

## FULTON IN BRITAIN

The switch had come at the behest of Fulton's friend and fellow inventor, the Earl of Stanhope. Like Fulton, he had designed a steamboat, but his failed to run. Stanhope believed in the ability of Fulton's vessels to plant mines, and he had created a mine-sweeping device to find such mines so that they could be removed.

In Britain, Fulton's proposals received substantial government backing. Among his proposals was a submarine system, which included a plan for organizing special squadrons and going on the offensive.

Fulton's system consisted of explosive devices and a means of delivering them to targets. He called it the submarine system because he initially envisioned using an upgraded version of his submarine as the delivery vehicle. However, this idea failed to win approval. Therefore, Fulton agreed to make the explosive devices and deliver them by surface vessels. Today, we call his devices "mines." At the time, they were referred to as "submarine bombs," "coffers," "carcasses," or "torpedoes."

Fulton designed two types of mines. One was a floating version designed to anchor beneath the surface of the water and explode when a vessel came into contact with it. The other was a little bit heavier than water and had a clockwork mechanism that could be set on a sort of timer to control when it would explode. It was attached underwater to the anchor cable of an enemy vessel, and it had a cork float, which kept it from sinking too deep. The tide or a current would move the mine under the hull of the ship, and at the set time the clockwork mechanism would cause it to explode.

Fulton did run into some opposition to his system. Some of those who thought the mines would succeed were concerned that Britain's enemies could get their hands on them and build their own mines to be used against British ships. Others thought Fulton was a crackpot.

The first mines were copper spheres. A later type was a watertight box 21 feet (6.4 m) long, carrying forty barrels of gunpowder. Under cover of darkness, sailors dressed in dark clothes put the first mines in place using a catamaran.

## INVADING BRITAIN

In 1805, Napoleon attempted to test his naval plan to invade Britain. Before the flotilla could cross the English Channel, however, Napoleon had to gain control of it.

Napoleon's invasion idea started with luring away the British ships blockading the French ports. He planned to have the Brest fleet and the Franco-Spanish fleet in Toulon break through the British blockade and then sail toward the West Indies, hopefully drawing the British fleet after them in pursuit. The idea was that the two French fleets would meet at the island of Martinique, evade the pursuing British fleet, sail back to Europe, and defeat the part of the British fleet that remained in the English Channel. After that, they could defend the flotilla crossing to Britain.

The plan was daring but impractical. Only the Toulon fleet was able to break out, and, when it reached Martinique and didn't find the Brest fleet, it sailed back to Europe. There, the British fleet blockading Rochefort and Ferrol defeated it at the Battle of Cape Finisterre. The fleet was forced back into port, and Napoleon called off the naval invasion of Britain.

## PUTTING MINES TO USE

There were at least seven British attempts to use the mines between 1804 and 1805, and in some cases they exploded, but they failed to sink their target. The French did learn to be on the lookout for mines. The final attempt by the British to use Fulton's mines took place in November 1805, but this attempt failed as well, due to foul weather.

In 1806, after an argument with the British government about money, Fulton left Britain for the United States. He angrily predicted that there would come a day when Britain would find its coast and the English Channel choked with mines—but this would not ring true for over one hundred years.

Soldiers in a French army camp near Sevastopol during the Russian campaign.

# Canned Food

But from day to day hunger increased, and it became necessary for the regiment to requisition and slaughter livestock so that the men could have some meat in addition to the potatoes and grits which they found here and there. Bread was rare and there was nothing to buy." This quote from *The Diary of a Napoleonic Foot Soldier* by Jakob Walter, illustrates the difficulty that the average soldier in Napoleon's army had in finding adequate food while on the march—in this case through a village in Poland.

Despite Napoleon ordering provisions such as soup, boiled and roasted joints of meat, and some vegetables, soldiers were largely expected to forage for their own food, buying it from locals or scavenging for it in the countryside. This was because provisions did not always arrive at their destinations. Drivers of food-delivery vehicles, called supply wagons, had to contend with bad weather, poor roads, and other hazards that sometimes made it impossible to get items to all of the army regiments.

## FORAGING FOR FOOD

In western and central Europe, which was densely populated and well supplied with shops and traveling traders, there were a number of options for obtaining food. In camp, regimental bakeries supplied soldiers with a basic quantity of bread. The local population was required to provide food to the army, and units were designated to requisition food from the locals. Soldiers could buy additional food—and liquor—from canteen keepers (called sutlers), many of whom were women and often the wives of soldiers. Food could also be purchased from traveling tradesmen.

The purchasing process was not always legitimate. Officers were known to write receipts for requisitioned food that promised payment at a future date, but then never actually pay. Soldiers also resorted to stealing crops. This was technically forbidden, but officers looked the other way as long as pilfering did not turn into pillaging on a large scale.

As can be seen from the quote that opens this chapter, finding food was sometimes difficult, even in Europe, away from major cities. The problem of finding food was much more difficult for soldiers fighting in poor countries far from western Europe, such as Russia and Egypt. During Napoleon's Egyptian campaign in 1798, fifty-five thousand soldiers marched for three days from

Alexandria to Cairo in intense heat through arid land. Many had expected to be able to forage for food and discarded their army-supplied biscuits. However, they found no food and water, and many died of hunger and thirst. When they reached Cairo, where food was available, the frustrated soldiers looted the city.

Napoleon's Russian campaign in 1812 was similarly disastrous. The long supply lines that stretched across Russia were cut by Russian troops. In addition, when the Russians were forced to retreat from a battle, they destroyed crops, food, and other items that might be useful to the French army. This lack of food meant that large numbers of French soldiers died of starvation.

In *The Diary of a Napoleonic Foot Soldier*, Jakob Walter repeatedly describes the difficulty of finding adequate food. He says of the Russian campaign:

> *Daily the hardships increased, and there was no hope of bread. My colonel spoke to us once and said that we could hope for no more bread until we crossed the enemy border. The most anyone might get was a little lean beef, and hunger made it necessary to dig up the fields of potatoes already sprouting, which were, however, very sweet and almost inedible. One also heard everywhere that several men had already shot themselves because of hardship.*

# NICOLAS APPERT AND CANNING

In 1795, the French Directory, which ruled France, decided they needed to find a better way to ensure adequate supplies of food for soldiers. They offered a 12,000-franc prize (equal to one year's average salary) for anyone who could come up with a method for, and published work on, the preservation of all types of food. When Napoleon came to power in 1799, no one had solved the problem. Napoleon continued to offer the prize. In 1810, the government was still searching for the answer.

A chef named Nicolas Appert (1749–1841) rose to the challenge. Appert was the son of an innkeeper at Châlons-sur-Marne, France. He was interested in preserving food from an early age and learned to pickle foods and brew beer. Appert was apprenticed to a chef at the Palais Royal Hotel in Châlons, France, before moving to Paris and becoming a confectioner (a maker of pastries and candy). He devoted fourteen years to coming up with an answer that would win him the prize. Louis Pasteur (1822–1895) had yet to identify bacteria, so the cause of spoilage was unknown. Appert conducted his experiments via trial and error.

Appert began experimenting with ways to preserve food in the late eighteenth century. At first he, like others of his time, believed that food spoiled because air was present, so he performed many experiments designed to remove air from food. In the process of his experimentation, he found that heat would prevent spoilage. He heated foods to temperatures over 212 degrees Fahrenheit (100 degrees Celsius) in an autoclave (a device that applies steam

Nicolas Appert, French chef and inventor, changed the way that food was preserved, creating the canned-food industry.

under pressure to sterilize whatever is placed inside). This is the temperature at which water boils and is sufficient to kill the bacteria that causes spoilage. Appert observed that heating food this way helped preserve it, but he didn't know why, since this was fifty years before the discovery of microbes that cause spoilage. Nonetheless, he identified a method that would work. The process Appert discovered is called "canning," because the food is placed in a can, or container. The term "can" referred to any type of container, including those made of ceramic and glass.

Appert's process took a long time to achieve. First he placed the food in glass jars. He stoppered the jars loosely with corks. He then wrapped the bottles in canvas, immersed them in water, and heated them to boiling. After they were sufficiently heated, he removed them from the water and tightened the corks, then sealed the bottles with wax. The whole process took about five hours. Appert was able to show that his process would keep food from spoiling for a long time. Furthermore, it could be used to preserve a variety of foods, including soup, meat, juices, vegetables, jams, jellies, syrups, and even some dairy products.

In 1809, he submitted his method to the French government, claiming the prize. In January 1810, the government awarded it to him. The terms of the prize required him to publish his findings, so Appert wrote the first cookbook that explained how to can food in this new way, *Le Livre de tous les menages, ou l'art de conserver, pendant plusieurs années, toutes les substances animales et vègétales* (*The Art of Preserving All Kinds of Animal and Vegetable*

*Substances for Many Years*). In addition to the 12,000 francs he was awarded, he also received an award from the Societe d'Encouragement pour l'Industrie Nationale (Society for the Encouragement of National Industry).

Fifty years later, another French scientist, Louis Pasteur, would explain that microbes (microscopic organisms such as bacteria) caused food to spoil. Boiling killed the microbes, and sealing the boiled food kept new ones from getting in.

## APPERT'S LEGACY

Appert had opened a canning factory at Massy in 1804. He used his award from the French government to expand it. The factory continued operations until 1933. In the 1820s, Appert switched from glass to tin-plated steel cans. The use of metal rather than glass cans improved the durability of the product, which was desirable to the military.

Appert went on to invent other culinary processes and products, including the bouillon cube and a method to extract gelatin from bones without the need to use acid.

By the 1820s, canned food was available to the general public as well as the military. However, the process of making the cans and preserving the food was so time consuming that the resulting product was very expensive. Therefore, only well-off people could afford it. Further advances in canning over the ensuing decades would make canned food more appealing for both military and civilian use. Today, canned foods are found throughout the world, in grocery stores and homes.

# The Tin Can

Once the secret of preserving food was revealed, the British also pursued the technology and improved upon it. Glass containers have the obvious drawback of being easy to break. In 1810, Peter Durand, an English merchant, received a patent for preserving food in tin cans as well as glass and pottery containers. His method was to fill containers with raw vegetables or partially cooked meat products, then place a partially closed cap on them and heat them. His process was based on information he learned from a friend, the French inventor Philippe de Girard.

His patent states that immediately after heating, the jar was to be sealed airtight, which could be accomplished by using a cork plug, a screw cap with a rubber seal, and a variety of other means. Durand's goal was to achieve large-scale production. He wanted to be able to preserve food in bulk quantities for use by the navy. In practice, Durand exclusively preserved food in tin cans. His finished product was tested by the Royal Navy, which sailed with some of Durand's cans for four to six months. Upon the naval vessels' return, the contents of the cans were examined by members of the British Royal Society and the Royal Institution. They found the food to be completely preserved and edible.

In 1812, Durand sold his patent to two other Englishmen, Bryan Donkin and John Hall, for £1,000 rather than pursue commercial canning himself. They set up a canning factory, and by 1813 they were supplying the first canned goods to the British army. In 1818, Durand received a patent in the United States for his food preservation process using tin cans.

By 1812, army rations began to be preserved in tin cans, which made them easier to store and transport.

The Union Army used observation balloons, like this one at Fair Oaks, near Richmond, Virginia, in 1862, to view troop locations and activities.

# Aftermath

M any of the innovations invented during the Napoleonic
Wars, including balloon-based aerial surveillance, the
submarine, the steamboat, mines, and canned rations, played
a much larger role in wars that occurred during the nineteenth
century, including the Franco-Prussian War (1870–1871),
fought between France under Napoleon III and Prussia, and the
American Civil War (1861–1865). Some are still in use today.

## BALLOONS AT WAR

Louis-Napoleon Bonaparte (1808–1873), also known as
Napoleon III, nephew and heir of Napoleon I, was president
(1850–1852) of the Second French Republic and then emperor
(1852–1870) of the Second French Empire. He employed a corps

of balloons that performed aerial reconnaissance over battlefields both in 1859 in the Franco-Austrian War and in 1870 in the Franco-Prussian War.

By the time of the American Civil War (1861–1865), the use of balloons for battlefield observation had spread across the Atlantic Ocean. Both the Union and Confederate armies used balloons. The Union army created the Union Army Balloon Corps, which was under the command of Professor Thaddeus S. C. Lowe. Professor Lowe had the military balloons constructed of stronger material than that used by civilian ballooners. The balloons, which could rise 1,000 feet (305 m) in the air, were used for locating artillery and for general observation. They were able to observe troop movements miles away. The Union army employed balloons around Washington, DC; on the southern coast of the United Sates; and on some western rivers. They were used in major eastern campaigns, including the 1862 Peninsula Campaign, and the Battles of Fredericksburg and Chancellorsville in Virginia. The Confederates used balloons during the Seven Days Battles, which took place around Richmond, Virginia.

During the Civil War, city gas was used to inflate the balloons—when it could be accessed. To inflate balloons in remote areas, Professor Lowe constructed "inflation wagons," which used iron filings and diluted sulfuric acid to produce hydrogen gas to fill the balloons.

The largest balloons (*Union* and *Intrepid*) had a capacity of 32,000 cubic feet (906 cubic meters) of lifting gas and could carry five people. The medium-sized balloons, *Constitution* and *United States,* had 25,000-cubic-foot (708 cubic m) envelopes and could carry up to three people. *Washington* had a 20,000-cubic-foot (566 cubic m) bag and could carry two people. With a capacity of 15,000 cubic feet (425 cubic m) each, *Eagle* and *Excelsior* were single-passenger craft. Navy ships were used to transport balloons along the coast and down rivers to the points of battle.

In most cases, the balloons were tethered, like those used in Napoleon I's day. Professor Lowe created a visual signaling system, and staff in the basket could flash gestures to officers on the ground to provide immediate intelligence about the enemy.

## AIRSHIPS

In the nineteenth century, inventors continued to experiment with the production of a dirigible-style airship. They searched for ways to add propulsion to balloons. An Australian medical doctor, William Bland, displayed a model of an "atmotic airship" to the 1851 Great Exhibition in London. It was an oblong balloon powered by a steam engine that turned a pair of propellers underneath it. A year later, Henri Giffard piloted a steam-powered dirigible 17 miles (27 km), making him the first person to achieve flight in an engine-powered vehicle.

During the Franco-Prussian War, Dupuy de Lome, a French naval engineer, designed a navigable balloon driven by a propeller turned by eight men. The balloon was intended to replace those used during the Siege of Paris (1870–1871) for communication between the city and the countryside. However, by the time it was finished, the war had ended.

The first use of an internal **combustion engine** to power an airship was accomplished in 1872 by Paul Haenlein, a German engineer who used an engine that ran on natural gas to inflate the dirigible's envelope. In 1874, Georgia native Micajah Clark Dyer filed a patent for an "Apparatus for Navigating the Air." After a balloon gave the airship its initial lift, a combination of wings and paddle wheels provided propulsion and navigation capabilities. The ship could be guided by a rudder. In 1883, the first flight in an electric-powered dirigible was made by French chemist Gaston Tissandier, who used a Siemens electric motor for power.

The first dirigible with a metal envelope was produced in 1897 by the Hungarian-Croatian engineer David Schwarz. He built the envelope out of aluminum. The first of the Zeppelin dirigibles, the Luftschiff Zeppelin LZ1, was produced in 1900. The Zeppelins were the most famous and successful of the dirigibles.

In 1900, Henri Deutsch de la Meurthe, a wealthy French businessman, offered a prize of 50,000 francs (approximately $200,000 today) to anyone who could fly any type of aircraft from the chateau at the Parc de Saint-Cloud to the Eiffel Tower (roughly 7 miles, or 11 km) and back in thirty minutes. On October 19, 1901, Alberto Santos-Dumont, a wealthy Brazilian living in France, won the prize, flying a small semi-rigid dirigible. Santos-Dumont's success started a boom in airship development.

The first advertising airship was built by British aeronaut Stanley Spencer in 1902. It featured advertising for baby food on both sides of the envelope.

An American journalist, Walter Wellman, attempted the first flights to the North Pole in 1907 and 1909, and then tried to achieve the first transatlantic flight in 1910 and again in 1912. He flew an enormous airship built in France, called the *America*. For his final transatlantic flight attempt, the ship had a crew of six plus a stray cat Wellman brought along for luck. Luck wasn't enough, and they only made it 1,000 miles (1,609 km) across the Atlantic before they had to abandon the ship. The crew (and the cat) were rescued by a steamship. Wellman published his adventures in a book, *The Aerial Age: A Thousand Miles by Airship over the Atlantic Ocean*.

## SUBMARINES

The Napoleonic Wars weren't the only conflict during the Napoleonic era in which a military used submarines. Britain also became embroiled in the War of 1812 (1812–1815) against the United States. There are contemporary accounts of at least two US submarines being used during this conflict. The story of one was reported in the *New York Evening Post*. According to the article, the vessel set out to engage in battle in June 1814 but was grounded on the eastern end of Long Island, where it was destroyed by two British warships. The second was a submarine designed by Silas Clowden Halsey. In 1814, it sank in the harbor of New London, Connecticut, while trying to plant mines on a British warship.

Submarines were used by both the Union and the Confederacy during the Civil War. The first submarine used in the Civil War was built for the Union in 1861 by the French inventor Brutus de Villeroi. It was launched in 1862. Named the *Alligator*, it was 47 feet (14.3 m) long and propelled by oars. It was sent to Virginia to destroy a bridge on the Appomattox River and clear obstructions from the James River, but both rivers were too shallow to allow the *Alligator* to submerge. Then, the Union Army wanted to use it to destroy a Confederate ironclad warship named

This photo shows a replica of the H.L. *Hunley*.

Strategic Inventions of the Napoleonic Wars

the *Virginia II*. However, testing revealed that the *Alligator* lacked sufficient power and was too unwieldy. The *Alligator* was refitted with a screw propeller instead of the oar system, and in 1863 the boat was sent to assist in the capture of Charleston, South Carolina. While being towed south, it had to be cut loose during a storm off Cape Hatteras, North Carolina, and sank.

The Confederacy constructed small steam-powered submarines. They called these "Davids" after the biblical character of David, slayer of Goliath and eventual king of Israel. One of the Davids disabled the USS *New Ironsides* with a torpedo in 1863, but it failed to sink the vessel. The first submarine to succeed in sinking its target was the *Hunley*. It was 40 feet (12.2 m) long and was operated by a hand crank turned by eight men. In February 1864, it made a night attack on the USS *Housatonic* off Charleston and sank it.

## STEAMSHIPS

Development of steamships continued in Europe during the nineteenth century. In 1842, the Russian Ministry of the Navy established the Steamship Committee. Four steam-powered frigates were added to the Baltic Fleet. The British and French navies used steam-powered ships extensively during the Crimean War (1853–1856) and proved that wooden sail-powered warships were no match for more maneuverable steam-powered ones. Most of the Russian Black Sea and Baltic fleets were destroyed. After that time, steam-powered ships completely replaced sail-powered warships.

Britain remained at the forefront of naval innovation. In 1861, the British built the HMS *Warrior*. The ship was built of iron rather than wood. Its steam engines reached 14.5 knots (16.7 miles per hour, or 26.8 kilometers per hour), and the ship was armed with breech-loading artillery, an improvement on the older type of cannon that was loaded from the end.

Steamships made their way into civilian use as well. The Eastern Steam Navigation Company launched the *Great Eastern*, better known as the *Leviathan*, in 1858. It traveled a route from Great Britain to the Far East and Australia, navigating around the Cape of Good Hope.

Steamboats played an important role in the Civil War, too. Both armies used them to transport troops and supplies along rivers. They were also used to guard supply barges and attack troops. The US government owned ninety-one steamboats, and the Union army **quartermaster** used steamboats on western rivers. These boats were the primary transport mechanism for troops and supplies. Steamboats were even plated with tin and used in tactical operations. These boats were called "tinclads."

The Civil War Battle of Hampton Roads took place on March 9, 1862. The steamships *Merrimack* and *Monitor* engaged in a naval battle that marked the beginning of modern naval warfare. In addition to being steam-powered, the ships were heavily armored, giving them protection not provided to ordinary wooden ships. The *Merrimack* was an ordinary steam frigate that had been built in the North. It was salvaged by the Confederates from the Norfolk,

# The Napoleon Expedition

Steamboats also were used in small support expeditions in the Civil War. The Napoleon expedition marks the first time black troops engaged in battle. After the Emancipation Proclamation of 1863 declared the slaves in the Southern states free, the Union formed the Second Arkansas Regiment (African Descent), and an expedition sailed down the Mississippi in the steamboat *Pike* from Helena, Arkansas, to recruit additional troops for the regiment. The boat stayed near the bank of the Mississippi River, traveling south until it arrived near Napoleon, Arkansas, then turning north and returning. Along the way, the troops engaged in a number of inland raids. At Island No. 65, the regiment was attacked by a Confederate force. They beat back the Confederates.

When the expedition arrived back at Helena, it was declared a success, having brought back an additional 125 recruits plus 75 captured mules, 8 captured horses, and a significant amount of food.

This painting by Thomas C. Skinner shows the Civil War battle between the *Monitor* and the *Merrimack* at Hampton Roads, on March 9, 1962.

Virginia, naval yard. They cut away its upper hull and iron-plated it, renaming the ship the *Virginia*. The Union *Monitor* had been designed from the beginning as an armored steam-powered warship with a revolving turret.

On March 9, the two ships met in a dramatic battle. The *Virginia* hit the *Monitor*'s pilot house and drove it into shallow water, but the *Virginia* had to return to the navy yard because

Strategic Inventions of the Napoleonic Wars

it had a leak in its hull and was running low on ammunition. Neither side won a decisive victory. However, the battle proved the superior strength and maneuverability of armored steam-powered warships.

## THE SPREAD OF CANNED FOOD

Not long after the invention of the tin can, canned food spread beyond Europe. The first canning factory in America was established by Robert Ayars in 1812 in New York City. Ayars's factory preserved meat, oysters, fruits, and vegetables in tin-plated wrought-iron cans. The first canned product to gain widespread acceptance with the US public was canned condensed milk, introduced by Gail Borden in 1856. In 1884, John L. Mason patented the Mason jar, an affordable glass jar with a lid that created a vacuum seal, allowing the jar to be used for home canning.

In the nineteenth century, canned food provided a way for explorers as well as soldiers to carry provisions into inhospitable environments. Admiral Sir John Ross took canned food to the Arctic in 1829, and Sir John Franklin did the same in 1845. Franklin disappeared while attempting to navigate the Northwest Passage near the Canadian Arctic. An 1857 expedition looking for traces of Franklin's expedition, led by Captain (later Admiral) Leopold McLintock, found cans among the stores they discovered. When one of the cans was opened in 1939, the contents were found to still be edible.

Workers in a typical mid-nineteenth-century canning factory fill cans with food and solder them shut.

In the mid-1800s, canned food became a status symbol among the middle class in Europe because of its expense. Improved manufacturing processes relying on mechanization decreased the cost of canned food in the late 1800s. Innovations in the equipment used to make cans made it possible to produce small steel cans by machine, and the time to cook the food in the cans was reduced from six hours to thirty minutes. The lower cost combined with an increase in urban populations, as people left farms for factory jobs in cities, led to a significant increase in the demand for canned food.

The large wars of the nineteenth century with their massive armies, including the Crimean War between a coalition of European countries and Russia, the American Civil War, and the Franco-Prussian War, increased the demand for canned food. These wars also introduced canned food to a large number of working-class men.

Until the mid-nineteenth century, people typically shopped for food each day. However, as more and more people migrated to cities, where they worked long hours in factories, they eagerly sought a cheap form of food that they could store, rather than have to shop after a day of work. Companies such as Underwood, Heinz, Campbell, and Nestlé responded to this need. The variety of canned food expanded, and decorative labels adorned cans as canners competed for the attention of consumers. These trends would continue beyond the nineteenth century into the modern era.

The Virginia-class fast-attack
submarine during trials in the
Atlantic Ocean on April 7, 2012

# CHAPTER
# SEVEN

# Lasting Effects

irigibles, submarines, and canned foods continued to play a role in war and peace during the twentieth and twenty-first centuries. As societies advanced, these technologies also kept evolving, and improvements were added. However, their basic uses remained the same as when they were first designed and implemented during the Napoleonic Wars.

## AIRSHIPS IN WORLD WAR I

In the early twentieth century, dirigibles were used by the military for the first time. The Italian forces were the first to employ a dirigible, which was used for a bombing mission during the Italo-Turkish War in 1912.

In World War I, the Germans, French, and Italians used dirigibles for tactical bombing and scouting, although their bombing accuracy was not very good. Dirigibles were hard to shoot down with aircraft or antiaircraft fire. Shooting holes in them had little effect because the pressure in their envelopes was only slightly higher than that of the air around them. The British eventually developed ammunition that was **incendiary** or explosive so that airplanes could set them on fire or blow them up.

For combat, the British exclusively replied on airplanes. However, they used small airships for detecting and counteracting submarines and mines. In 1915, the British designed the Sea Scout (SS) class of blimp.

The first two dirigibles that the US military attempted to construct during World War I failed. The *Shenandoah*, whose design was based on the German Zeppelin, flew successfully in 1923. By the end of World War I, airplanes replaced dirigibles as bombers, and both the British and Germans abandoned their military airship programs.

A number of countries, including Britain and the United States, continued to build passenger airships in the years between World War I and World War II. On July 2, 1919, the British R34 airship attempted to make a double crossing of the Atlantic between England and the United States. It successfully reached Mineola, Long Island, on July 6 and completed its return trip by July 8. It was the first such trip by an aircraft.

In 1925, the Larno Treaties released Germany from the restrictions on airship construction that had been imposed after World War I. The Zeppelin company began constructing the *Graf*

*Zeppelin*, the largest passenger airship the company had ever built, and it was a great success.

Both the British military and the US Navy experimented with using dirigibles as airborne aircraft carriers, carrying fighter planes. They built some experimental models, but the development of the seaplane ended the projects.

When the Empire State Building was built in 1931, a dirigible mast was installed for airship passenger service. Indeed, in the 1930s, the German Zeppelins competed successfully with other means of transportation, being outfitted much like airborne ocean liners. In 1937, however, the Zeppelin *Hindenburg* burst into flames and crashed as it was in the process of landing in New Jersey. The accident destroyed the public's faith in travel by dirigible and ended airship flights.

The airship *Hindenburg* exploded into a huge ball of fire as it came in for a landing at Lakehurst, New Jersey, in 1937. Luckily, many of the passengers and crew aboard managed to escape unharmed.

# AIRSHIPS IN WORLD WAR II AND BEYOND

When the Japanese and German submarines began sinking American ships along the coast in World War II, the US Navy remembered the usefulness of airships against submarines in World War I. The navy requested anti-submarine airships, and in 1942, two airship units were created—one based in Lakehurst, New Jersey, and the other in Sunnyvale, California. The major mission was to escort ship **convoys**. In the event of an attack, the airships targeted submarines with depth charges, forcing them to dive to depths that put them out of reach of their adversary. Under this program, only one ship escorted by an airship was sunk. This was a marked improvement compared to 532 that suffered without an airship escort. The airships themselves were also mostly without casualties. Just one was recorded as being forced down by an enemy submarine in 1943, primarily because the airship's depth charges failed to deploy.

Because of their utility in dealing with submarines, the US Navy used airships in Europe to find and destroy German U-boats around the Strait of Gibraltar. Airships also carried out search-and-rescue missions, and patroled the Caribbean. Altogether, US airships made 37,554 flights, flying a total of 378,237 hours during the war.

Today, dirigibles and blimps are no longer used for transportation. However, they are still used for other purposes, such as advertising. Since the 1920s, the Goodyear Tire and Rubber Company has maintained a fleet of blimps used for advertising, and "the Goodyear blimp" can still be seen in the skies above major sporting events.

Airships are also used in modern research. In 1993, the Per Lindstrand company built the world's largest thermal airship for French botanists who wanted a vehicle that could be positioned above the tree canopy of rain forests. Airships are also still being used by many countries for military surveillance missions. However, they are prone to mishaps every so often. In October 2015, a US military surveillance blimp escaped its moorings in Maryland and flew for hours over the East Coast, eventually coming to rest in Pennsylvania.

## SUBMARINES IN THE EARLY TWENTIETH CENTURY

In April 1900, the US Navy commissioned its first modern submarine, the USS *Holland*. By this time, submarines ran on a combustion engine on the surface and on electric battery power when submerged. Navies all around the world were commissioning similar submarines.

Not surprisingly, at the start of World War I, the British Royal Navy had the largest submarine service, consisting of seventy-four boats. The German Imperial Navy commissioned its first U-boat, *U-1*, in 1906. By the start of World War I, it had twenty-nine functional submarines and was in the process of constructing another forty-eight. The U-boats saw their first action in the First Battle of the Atlantic (1914–1918). The German navy engaged in extensive submarine warfare, using its U-boats to sink ships.

During the war, Germany built 380 subs, but almost half were lost in the course of the war. In 1915, a U-boat was used to sink the RMS *Lusitania*, a British civilian ocean liner sailing from New York to Liverpool, England. This act played a key role in bringing the United States into World War I because 128 of the passengers killed in the attack were American.

## THE SUBMARINE IN WORLD WAR II

At the end of World War I, Germany was forced to sign the Treaty of Versailles, which among other things limited the size of the German military. Therefore, the Germans only began seriously bolstering their forces a year before the beginning of World War II. They couldn't hope to build enough battleships to challenge the British navy, so they concentrated on building a substantial submarine fleet to use to sink British ships. By the end of the war, the German navy had a thousand submarines. In the Second Battle of the Atlantic (1939–1945), fought around the British Isles, the submarines devastated British ships, although they failed to keep US and Canadian supplies from getting to Britain.

When the Japanese attacked the US Pacific fleet at Pearl Harbor on December 7, 1941, many of the navy's surface ships were destroyed. However, the submarines survived. They were immediately rallied to hunt and sink Japanese ships. Representing only 2 percent of the US Navy, the submarine service took out more than 30 percent of the Japanese navy, as well as 60 percent of the Japanese merchant fleet.

## Steamships

Charles Parsons (1854–1931), a British engineer, founded the Parsons Marine Turbine Company to provide engines for ships. He developed the steam turbine engine for his yacht, the *Turbinia*, in 1897. The engine gave the yacht a speed of 34 knots (39 miles per hour, or 63 kilometers per hour), 7 knots faster than the top naval vessels at the time. Within two years, the Royal Navy was building ships with the Parsons steam turbine engine, and shortly thereafter, ocean liner companies started using it in passenger ships.

In World Wars I and II, most naval vessels were driven by steam turbine engines. Thousands of Liberty Ships with steam-piston-driven engines and Victory Ships with steam turbine engines were used during World War II.

Even today, large naval ships and submarines are powered by steam turbines. Nuclear-powered submarines use such engines, relying on nuclear reactors to boil water to produce steam to drive the vessels. The first commercial (nonmilitary) nuclear-powered vessel was the NS *Savannah*. It was built in the 1950s to demonstrate the utility of nuclear power as a fuel for ships carrying passengers and cargo. In the 1970s, the Sea-Land Service bought eight steam-powered cargo ships, which are still the world's fastest cargo vessels. They were sold to the US Navy in the early 1980s. Companies such as Mitsubishi Heavy Industries and Hyundai Heavy Industries still build steam-powered cargo ships, including carriers for transporting liquid natural gas. Thus, there is no sign that the construction of steam-powered vessels will stop anytime soon.

## MODERN SUBMARINES

In 1955, the United States launched the first nuclear-powered submarine, the USS *Nautilus*. Other countries soon followed suit. Simultaneously, equipment was invented that allowed the extraction of oxygen from seawater, enabling submarines to stay submerged for months. Most US submarines today use nuclear power. In 2000, the *Virginia*-class submarine was commissioned. This most recent class of US subs is designed with enhanced stealth, surveillance, and weapons capabilities so that it can be used for a wide range of missions.

## THE EVOLUTION OF CANNED FOOD

The techniques of canning that were developed in the nineteenth century had a profound effect on the preparation of food in both military and civilian applications in the twentieth and twenty-first centuries.

The canned meat and vegetables supplied to the British navy in the nineteenth century were the ancestors of special military rations first used in the twentieth century. Until the 1900s, the primary type of military-supplied food was the "garrison ration," food supplied in bulk to feed large numbers of soldiers in a single location. The US military first recognized the need to issue rations that could be carried by individual soldiers in 1901, after the Spanish-American War. The army identified five situations in which troops might operate, each requiring a different type of

ration. These were: in a garrison, in the field, traveling overland, on naval vessels, and under emergency conditions.

World War I involved millions of soldiers deployed across the world. The need to feed these vast armies created an enormous demand for canned food. Commanders everywhere needed high-calorie food that could be transported long distances in all climates at an affordable price. Initially, soldiers were fed canned corn beef, pork and beans, and canned sausages. However, by 1916, in an attempt to improve morale, militaries starting purchasing more appetizing and meal-like food. Items such as canned ravioli and spaghetti began to appear. After the war, the companies that had supplied canned food to the military switched over to offering their canned food as a convenience product to the general public. This created an even bigger emphasis on making canned food appetizing.

In 1920, the US Quartermaster School was established, as well as the Quartermaster Subsistence Research and Development Laboratory (now the Quartermaster Food and Container Institute for the Armed Forces), to design appropriate rations for troops. These included Field Ration B, which consisted of canned food to be used to feed troops in the field, and Field Ration C, a packaged ration containing a complete set of food for one day, to be carried by individual soldiers.

During World War II, the use of aircraft and mechanized vehicles allowed soldiers to be deployed in a wide variety of terrains and climates. This exacerbated the need for individual rations that could be carried by soldiers traveling rapidly. Examples of canned rations used during World War II include instant coffee, hash, meat and noodles, meat and beans, chili, stew, spaghetti, canned chicken, canned ham, and most famously, Spam. These products are still commercially available. Spam, which has become a pop-cultural byword for "mystery meat," is a form of highly processed pork shoulder combined with potato starch, salt, sugar, water, and sodium nitrate (as a preservative). Extremely high in fat and salt, and not to everyone's taste, the product was sometimes used for purposes other than food, such as a source of grease for lubrication.

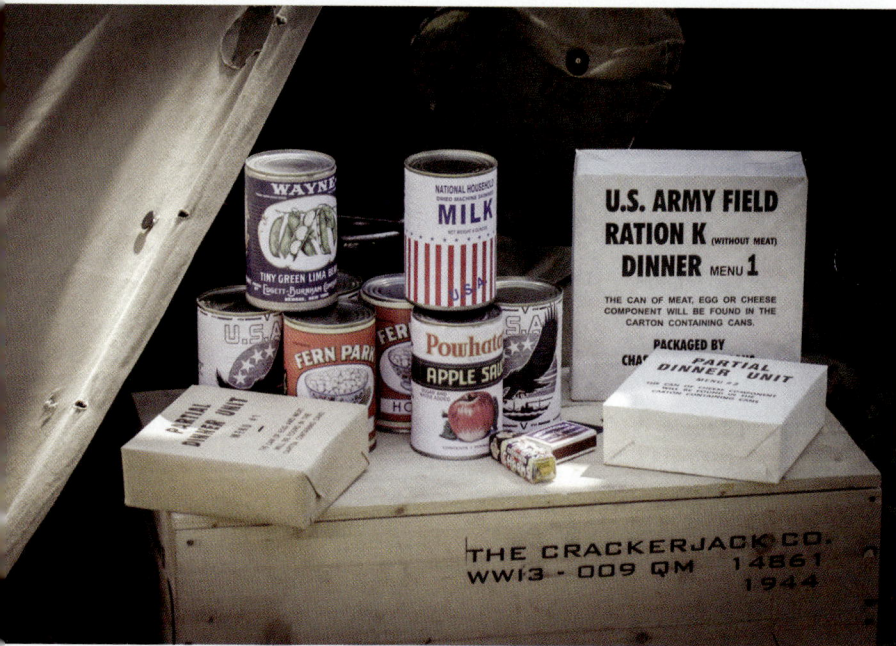

Typical canned and K rations issued by the US military during World War II, including a variety of canned food

Strategic Inventions of the Napoleonic Wars

During World War II, a large number of women entered the workforce while many men were away fighting. Rationing, which limited the availability of fresh food, combined with the need for a quick, convenient way to prepare food, fueled the demand for canned food in America's kitchens.

From the 1950s until the mid-1970s, canned rations called C rations were issued to troops who were in environments where group cooking was not possible. In 1981, meals ready to eat (MREs), which consisted of packaged food in packets, replaced canned rations for US soldiers in the field.

In the 1950s, the hot wars of the 1940s gave way to the Cold War, a nuclear standoff between the United States and the Soviet Union, both of which had developed nuclear weapons in the post–World War II period. Two major trends increased the demand for canned food in the 1950s. First, despite public relations efforts after World War II to get women to leave the workforce and give their jobs back to men, many women continued to work. In addition, the creation of new desirable but expensive consumer goods, such as cars and televisions, led many married women to continue to work so that a family could use the additional income to buy high-ticket items. Therefore, convenience foods, including canned and frozen dinners, replaced fresh food that required time-consuming preparation. Second, many people feared that a nuclear war would break out between the United States and the Soviet Union. In response, some people stored large stocks of canned food in case such a disaster occurred.

## FOOD IN THE TWENTY-FIRST CENTURY

The first aluminum can was produced by Alcoa in 1957. Aluminum cans had the advantages of being easier and cheaper to manufacture, not requiring the lid to be soldered to the can, not rusting, and being recyclable. In 2004, cans with easy-to-open lids were introduced, and two years later, single-serving metal cans appeared. Today, Americans use more than 130 million cans annually, and the can-making industry employs thirty-five thousand people.

The period of the Napoleonic Wars was the dawn of the modern industrial era. Many innovations introduced during that period changed the nature of both warfare and civilian life. They have continued to improve in the two centuries that followed, and will likely continue to evolve into new forms in the future.

Today, many modern shoppers can find canned food in grocery stores.

# GLOSSARY

**abdicate**  To give up a throne.

**amalgam**  A combination or blend.

**aristocrat**  A member of the nobility.

**artillery**  A cannon or other large gun that fires projectiles.

**blimp**  A non-rigid airship.

**blockade**  To block access to a harbor or port.

**coalition**  A union of countries or groups.

**combustion engine**  An engine that uses oxygen to burn a fuel such as gasoline.

**consulate**  A type of government headed by a small number of chief executives, known as consuls.

**Continental System**  A system put in place by Napoleon in which the countries under his control agreed not to buy goods from Britain.

**convoy**  A group of vehicles traveling together.

**coup d'état**  The overthrowing of a government.

**dirigible**  An airship with a rigid structure.

**exile**  To banish a person from his or her country.

**flotilla**  A group of small naval vessels.

**forage**  To search for food.

**Iberian Peninsula** The area on the west coast of Europe that consists of Spain and Portugal.

**ignite** To set on fire.

**impasse** A stalemate.

**incendiary** Able to start a fire.

**Piedmontese** A person or object from Piedmont, Italy.

**prosperity** The state of being well-off.

**prowess** Skill.

**quartermaster** An officer responsible for providing troops with food, clothing, housing, fuel, and the like.

**republic** A form of government in which the people elect representatives to govern the country.

**rhetoric** The art of using language to influence people.

**rudder** A device attached to the bottom of a ship that allows the person sailing it to adjust the ship's direction.

**subordinates** People who report to someone with more authority.

**tether** To tie down.

**undermine** To sabotage or injure someone by underhanded means.

# BIBLIOGRAPHY

Bruce, Robert B., Iain Dickie, Kevin Kiley, Michael F. Pavkovic, and
Frederick C. Schneid. *Techniques of the Napoleonic Age: 1792–1815:
Equipment, Combat Skills, and Tactics*. New York: St. Martin's
Press, 2008.

Busch Systems. "A Brief Timeline of Recycling."
Retrieved June 19, 2016. http://www.buschsystems.com/recycling-
bin-news/2014/05/a-brief-timeline-of-the-history-of-recycling.

Can Manufacturers Institute. "History of the Can: An Interactive
Timeline." Retrieved June 19, 2016. http://www.cancentral.com/
can-stats/history-of-the-can.

Century of Flight. "The Use of Military Balloons in the Napoleonic Era."
Retrieved June 8, 2016. http://www.century-of-flight.net/new%20
site/balloons/Napoleonic.htm.

Civil War Trust, The. "Civil War Ballooning." Retrieved June 16, 2016.
http://www.civilwar.org/education/history/civil-war-ballooning/
civil-war-ballooning.html?referrer=https://www.google.com.

Cowdy, T. E. *Napoleon's Infantry Handbook: An Essential Guide to Life in
the Grand Army*. South Yorkshire, UK: Pen & Sword Military, 2015.

Dash, Mike. "The Secret Plot to Rescue Napoleon by Submarine."
*Smithsonian*, March 8, 2013. http://www.smithsonianmag.com/
history/the-secret-plot-to-rescue-napoleon-by-submarine-
1194764/?no-ist.

Dwyer, Phillip. *Napoleon: The Path to Power*. New Haven, CT: Yale University Press, 2009.

Ellis, Geoffrey. *Studies in History: The Napoleonic Empire*. New York: Palgrave, 2003.

Encyclopedia Britannica. "Coup of 18–19 Brumaire." Retrieved May 29, 2016. http://www.britannica.com/event/Coup-of-18-19-Brumaire.

———. "French Revolutionary and Napoloenic Wars." Retrieved April 20, 2016. http://www.britannica.com/event/French-revolutionary-wars.

Encyclopedia of World Biography. "Nicolas Appert." 2004. http://www.encyclopedia.com/topic/Nicolas_Appert.aspx.

Gratzer, Walter. *Terrors of the Table: The Curious History of Nutrition*. New York: Oxford University Press, 2005.

Harris, Brayton. "World Submarine Timeline Part One: 1580–1869." Retrieved June 9, 2016. http://www.submarine-history.com/NOVAone.htm.

History Channel. "The First Parachutist." Retrieved June 9, 2016. http://www.history.com/this-day-in-history/the-first-parachutist.

———. "Napoleon Bonaparte." Retrieved May 22, 2016. http://www.history.com/topics/napoleon.

*History Wings* Magazine. The French Aerostatic Corps. April 2, 2013. http://fly.historicwings.com/2013/04/the-french-aerostatic-corps.

MacDonald, Janet. *Feeding Nelson's Army. The True Story of Food at Sea in the Georgian Era*. South Yorkshire, UK: Chatham, 2014.

Markham, David J. "The Revolution, Napoleon, and Education."
International Napoleon Society. Retrieved June 22, 2016. http://
www.napoleon-series.org/research/society/c_education.html.

Martyris, Nina. "Appetite for War: What Napoleon and His Men Ate on
the March." National Public Radio, June 18, 2015. http://www.npr.
org/sections/thesalt/2015/06/18/414614705/appetite-for-war-
what-napoleon-and-his-men-ate-on-the-march.

Neumann, Caryn E. "Steamboats (Civil War)." Encyclopedia of
Arkansas History and Culture. Accessed June 17, 2016. http://
www.encyclopediaofarkansas.net/encyclopedia/entry-detail.
aspx?entryID=6437.

Poore, Devon. "Civil War Submarines." New York Times, January 27, 2015.

US Department of State Office of the Historian. "The Napoleonic
Wars and the United States, 1803–1815." Retrieved May 20, 2016.
https://history.state.gov/milestones/1801-1829/napoleonic-wars.

US Quartermaster Foundation. "Army Operational Rations – Historical
Background." Retrieved June 19, 2016. http://www.qmfound.com/
army_rations_historical_background.htm.

Walter, Jakob. Diary of a Napoleonic Foot Soldier. Edited by Marc Raeff.
New York: Doubleday, 1991.

# FURTHER INFORMATION

## Websites

**EmperorNapoleon.com: Maps of Europe During the Napoleonic Wars**
http://emperornapoleon.com/maps
This website shows a series of maps illustrating how Europe changed over the course of the Napoleonic Wars.

**Military Heritage: The Napoleonic Wars**
http://www.militaryheritage.com/napoleon.htm
Military Heritage provides articles, sound clips, military replicas, and more.

**The Napoleonic Guide: The Campaigns of Napoleon 1792–1815**
http://www.napoleonguide.com/campind.htm
The Napoleonic Guide provides detailed information on each of Napoleon's campaigns.

**War Times Journal: Napoleonic War Series**
http://www.wtj.com/wars/napoleonic
*War Times Journal* provides a range of articles on the Napoleonic Wars.

## Videos

**Empires: Napoleon**

This PBS Home Video production describes Napoleon's rise, accomplishments, campaigns, and exile.

**Living the French Revolution and the Age of Napoleon**

A twenty-five part series by The Teaching Company covering various events, people, and military campaigns. (Available as individual episodes from Amazon.com as well as on DVD.)

**Napoleon**

This A&E Biography covers Napoleon's background, political career, and military exploits.

# INDEX

# ABOUT THE AUTHOR

**Jeri Freedman** has a BA from Harvard University. She worked for a number of years in the education department of the Anti-Defamation League in programs providing information on the Holocaust to history teachers. She then worked for fifteen years at high-technology companies. She is the author of more than fifty young adult nonfiction books, including *Tech in the Trenches: Strategic Inventions of World War II, A Documentary History of the Holocaust: The Warsaw Ghetto and Uprising,* and *Tech in the Trenches: Strategic Inventions of the French Revolution.*